The Process Of Becoming

Sylvia Fleming

Foreword by Sarah Morgan

Published in the United States by
Morgan Publishing, Los Angeles, CA

Paper Back ISBN 978-15136-6758-4

DEDICATION

I dedicate this book to:

Abba God for walking me through this season of my life. Chapter by chapter, He reminded me that I had to finish and finish strong *to become* and write this book. Thank you for the encouragement, affirmations, confirmations, and even the instructions to help me press past every opposition. Thank you for never leaving or forsaking me.

To my daddy, Richard L. Fleming, *my hero*. Thank you for not abandoning your seed, for always being there for us. Thank you for giving of yourself sacrificially and unselfishly. Thank you for believing in me and encouraging me to do and be my best self. I even thank you for my early childhood *whoopings*. They worked. They did not kill me; they helped make me. Thank you.

To my siblings, Michael, Grenae, Rhonda,

Tiffany, Racquel, Rochelle, and our plus one, our cousin-sister, Veronica, thank you guys for your love and support, prayers, and your presence when I needed it most. Thank you for hosting Champ on nights I needed to write. Thank you even for the disagreements we had that ultimately caused us to deepen our love for one another. You are appreciated.

To all who have played a part in my *becoming*—good or bad, thank you!

Lastly, to my son, Derrick D. Hicks, at one point, you asked me, "What would I do if...?" Well, we are doing it. I just wish you were here to do it with us. Rest well, honey.

CONTENTS

ACKNOWLEDGMENTS

I give honor to Jehovah God Almighty for walking me through this *process.* Thank you for inspiring and teaching me every step of the way. THANK YOU, FATHER.

To Pastor Calvin and Apostle Veronica Moore, thank you for believing in me, supporting me, encouraging, and pushing me into *pu*rpose. I am forever grateful. THANK YOU.

To Bishop William and Dr. Sarah Morgan for helping develop in me the stamina, strategies, and insights needed to know how to navigate life and ministry. Thank you for helping me *command my morning,* day, and night. Thank you for teaching me to own the scriptures. Your yes to God helped transform my life. THANK YOU.

To Dr. Wanda Davis, you demonstrated strength, courage, transparency, grace, class, wisdom, and a sense of humor that is out of this world. Thank you for the Women's Fellowships where you gave us *Pillow Talk* to equip us for the Dos and Don'ts of ministry and marriage. Thank you for the many impartations that I continue to draw from after many years. THANK YOU.

To Prophetess Karla, *Coach K~,* Allen, for your coaching skills and for keeping me on track to walk in a spirit of excellence in more ways than you ever know. THANK YOU.

To Pastor Rochelle Hess, Evangelist Gwendolyn Collins, and Evangelist Evelyn Nixon, for your love, support, and intercession, THANK YOU.

To Clint D. Johnson, for your poem "Eye the Butterfly," which captured everything I dropped. THANK YOU for picking it up.

FOREWORD

As I read Lady Sylvia's memoir, I was instantly taken back to a hot summer Thursday night Trees of Righteousness mentoring class. That night I started to teach what was meant to be a three-week series on the subject "Change." It lasted over two months as I meticulously and thoroughly plowed through the Word of God using the parallel life process of how a caterpillar *becomes* a beautiful butterfly.

> *"I APPEAL to you, therefore, brethren, and beg of you in view of [all] the mercies of God, to make a decisive dedication of your bodies [presenting all your members and faculties] as a living sacrifice, holy (devoted, consecrated) and well-pleasing to God, which is your reasonable (rational, intelligent) service*

and spiritual worship. Do not be conformed to this world (this age), [fashioned after and adapted to its external, superficial customs], but ***be transformed (changed)*** *by the [entire] renewal of your mind [by its new ideals and its new attitude], so that you may prove [for yourselves] what is the good and acceptable and perfect will of God, even the thing which is good and acceptable and perfect [in His sight for you]" Romans 12:1-2 [AMPC].*

The word *transformed* comes from the Greek word *metamorphosis. Metamorphosis* is a process in which a caterpillar undergoes extreme physical and internal changes that occur within a particular time after birth. The result of metamorphosis changes the organism's entire bodily makeup, whereby the butterfly looks nothing like a caterpillar. Thus, metamorphosis is a miraculous process.

The metamorphosis process involves a re-activating of genes that allow the cells to change from one cell type to another and is triggered by hormones, which the animal's body releases as conditions for a metamorphosis approach. These hormones cause drastic changes to cells' functioning and even behavioral changes such as the caterpillar *becoming* a chrysalis, the hard-shelled pupa of the butterfly, a protected stage of development known as the cocoon. Likewise, as we are *processed to become*, we go through the four stages of metamorphosis:

1 **THE DERIVATION OF LIFE** - The Cocoon, eating-feeding stage. The butterfly, which starts as a worm-like, leaf-eating caterpillar, transforms into a flying, nectar-drinking beautiful creature with an exoskeleton, is the *process of beco*ming.

2 **THE DRAWING OF GOD** - The Transition stage is the stage in which He draws us.

3 **THE DELIVERANCE OF THE BUTTERFLY** - The reproduction and maturation stage.

4 **THE DUPLICATION OF THE BUTTERFLY** - The procreation stage, whereby we *become* and do what we are called to do—helping others.

The Process of Becoming is Lady Sylvia's personal narration of those four stages. I love how Isaiah 41:10 puts it in the Amplified version. He suggests that the *process of becoming* strengthens and hardens us to difficulties that cause us to emerge bold and beautiful.

> *"Fear not [there is nothing to fear], for I am with you; do not look around you in terror and be dismayed, for I am your God.* **I will strengthen and harden you to difficulties,** *yes, I will help you; yes, I will hold you up and retain you with My [victorious] right hand of rightness and justice" (Isaiah 41:10).*

As you join Lady Sylvia on her journey and *process of becoming* presented with simplicity, authenticity, and transparency; you will discover that the dark, lonely, slimy, and humiliating parts of metamorphosis are hidden from the view of most people because it is a personal process that is preparing the unique you.

In the cocoon, the caterpillars do not merely gain legs, wings, and an exoskeleton; they also grow new eyes (recovery of sight), lose their leaf-eating mouthparts (appetite change), replace them with nectar-sucking proboscises, and gain mature reproductive organs.

The Process of Becoming is the reproduction phase of Lady Sylvia selflessly sharing her *process of becoming* with principles that you can pull from no matter where you are in your *process of becoming*, knowing that with prayer, faith, trust, and confidence in God, you too will *become*.

As you read *The Process of Becoming*, you will find yourself as I did, having a heart-to-heart conversation with Lady Sylvia; you will laugh, cry, get mad, ponder, even be triggered in some areas, but most importantly, you will be inspired and motivated to stay in the *process to become*.

Thank you, Lady Sylvia, for sharing. You have genuinely *become*, and I am proud to call you, daughter.

Sarah Morgan
Prayer Academy Global
Los Angeles, California

INTRODUCTION

From the beginning of my conception, the hand of the LORD has been on my life. God knew me before I was a seed in my mother's womb. There was a plan and purpose in God's mind for my life even before my daddy met my mother. God purposed for me to be the fourth born, middle child into the family of Lady Rosie Lee and Mr. Richard Lee Fleming, and He knew then why He afforded me the privilege of life. He spoke over me, and I became a living soul. At the command of His voice, my life sparked a reaction from the enemy of my soul to oppose God's plans for my life.

Upon my arrival, there were announcements made on the earth that troubled the enemy's camp. Simultaneously, the enemy made inquiries and collected data to oppose (kill, steal, and destroy) God's plans and purpose for my life. Like so, please understand that the enemy uses whatever he can to distract, discourage, and disqualify you from *becoming* God's original intent for your life is worth the sacrifice.

The devil prowls around like a roaring lion looking to quickly devour, demolish, eat up quickly, consume, or shift your focus to destroy your destiny. He desires to sift you as wheat, subtract from you, and take you from a state of wholeness to a state of lack and devastation. He aims to make a whole person fragile, weak, and humiliated to undermine your ability and strength to stay together and function as the solid unit God created you to *become*.

Nevertheless, thank God for Jesus Christ, who continually intercedes and pleads to God on your behalf for mercy, clemency, and leniency so you can escape the plans of the enemy. God gives grace so that you can continue to move forward, walk in faith, and believe that what God has said about you, He can also bring it to pass as you stay connected to Him, the True Vine and Source of your strength, to progress and *become*.

The Process of Becoming will not be your everyday Christian read. Sequentially, I will take you through part of my journey for you to see the various tactics used by the enemy to try to deter and derail me from *becoming*. As you *become* a witness to a portion of my life, it will help you identify some of the tactics the enemy uses against you in an attempt to derail your destiny. *Let the process begin*.

CHAPTER 1

THE COCOON STAGE

At birth, I was this beautiful, brown-eyed, curly-haired, bouncing baby girl, my granny's namesake, whom everyone seemed to love. As I grew up, we would visit our relatives' homes, and I began to take notice of all of the baby pictures of my little face in our huge family photo albums. Later on, down the line, I saw full-body shots of myself. Seeing those pictures, I realized then that I was living a protected life.

I was born with a severe case of genu varum (bowlegs). As a result, I was in leg casts for quite some time to straighten them out before I could finally start walking. Imagine being a toddler with those itchy, white casts on both legs with a bar connecting them and being carried around everywhere while every other little person was playing and running around everywhere. Even now, I can remember the sadness I felt from being left out while my family and friends played.

It was not until I was about two-and-half-years old before my feet could finally hit the ground, and boy oh boy, did I hit the ground running. I ran and ran and ran, like a jackrabbit running from its hunter. I ran around chairs, tables, in driveways, around people, and anything I could squeeze by. Until one day, I was running in one of my aunts' houses around her 1970's hardwood coffee table that had pointed ends. I ran around the table, playing with my cousin, who is a year younger than me. Suddenly, I tripped, and I fell face forward, hitting the center of my forehead on the pointed end of the table. Instead of me running around, I was confined again due to the blood that was running down my face from the gash on my forehead. My family grabbed towels and whatever else they could find, attempting to s the bleeding. They quickly learned from the frantic 911 call that putting pressure on the wound would stop the bleeding if the injury was not too bad or life-threatening. Thank God it was not.

Although I have a permanent *scar,* it definitely could have been worse. Even so, I embrace the scar as it reminds me of God's hand of protection and the promise of His Word in Isaiah 54:17 that says,

> *"No weapon that is formed against thee shall prosper, and every tongue that shall rise against thee in judgment thou shalt condemn. This is the heritage of the servants of the LORD, and their righteousness is of Me, saith the LORD."*

Not many months later, my mom and I and one of her eight sisters and her daughter were in a terrible car accident. We were blindsided and rear-ended by another car. I remember it like it was yesterday. We were stopped at a stop sign in my dad's new white Grand Prix with the white trim around the tires and crushed velvet burgundy interior, then, BOOM! Suddenly, we plunged forward, and the sound of crushing metal and breaking glass caused fear and panic to grip us. Once we gathered ourselves from the shock of what happened, we realized that the impact caused my mom to hit her face against the steering wheel. The force of the collision almost severed my mom's bottom lip, and we could see then that she had even lost a tooth or two.

Shattered glass fragments left a large gash in my aunt's arm, of which the scar is still visible today. As with me, the mark serves as a daily reminder of God’s hand of protection and how He spared our lives that day.

The accident shook up my baby cousin. We were all taken to the hospital, by ambulance, for observation; at two-and-half years old, doctors noted her as being one of the youngest cases ever to be diagnosed with diabetes. Although

everything was out of whack for h
extended His kindness and mercy to h

As for me, the impact almost threw me from the car. Tossed like a ragdoll from the backseat and partially thrown out of a window, I lost consciousness momentarily. I regained consciousness to the sounds of shaking and shattering tiny pieces of glass falling inside the car. Although the car was totaled, by the grace of God, we all survived the accident.

There are times in life when things will happen to you show you what matters in life. In those times, you must learn to realize that God does allow some things to happen. He will let your *Uzziah* die (Isaiah 6:1), your property go into foreclosure, your idols fall, and your *Saul*s turn on and *betray* you to *preserve* the *purpose* on the inside of you (I Samuel 18:31). He will also allow some *scars* to remain visible as reminders of His presence with you in seasons of misfortune.

The following two scriptures come to mind

as additional *reminders* of God's hand of protection. His constant hand of mercy and protection is available to us even now.

> *"Be strong and of a good courage, fear not, nor be afraid of them: for the LORD thy God, He it is that doth go with thee; He will not fail thee, or forsake thee" (Deuteronomy 31:6).*

> *"And we know that all things work together for good to them that love God, to them who are called according to His purpose" (Romans 8:28).*

Shout hallelujah to God for not allowing the plans of the enemy to succeed against you. Thank God for His hand blocking every opposition. Give Him praise for your battle scars. You survived!

At age five, as a helpless kindergartener, while outside playing in the front yard of our apartment, a man approached a group of us, saying that he "needed help finding his lost dog." The male lured us away and convinced two of us to go with him. We were taken three to four blocks away from home, behind a ruddy, green apartment building (which is still the same ruddy, green apartment building today.) I was held at *gunpoint* and told, "You better not scream or make a noise!"

The incident was yet another trauma and, by far, the scariest situation I had ever experienced. At that moment, everything seemed to go dark, and the moment seemed to unfold in slow motion. Shaking, nervous, sweating, and scared out of my mind, I stood there helplessly frozen. The threatening words of the perpetrator prevented me from crying or making a sound. Silently, I was trying to figure out if we would live or die in my young mind. Until finally, we were let go.

In the same way, in the early stages of your life, where helplessness and naivety are present, the enemy of your soul will forcibly attempt to take advantage of you by creating events that plant seeds and paint pictures in your minds, which produce thoughts designed to breed a lifestyle contrary to God's original intent for your life. This stage is where you need more seasoned, discerning, and wise people in your life who not only want to protect you but can also see what God has placed on the inside of you. It would help if you had people who could redirect you mentally, emotionally, psychologically, and spiritually during this phase.

After that horrific incident, my mother grew closer to God. We began going to my cousin's grandfather's church, my uncle Junebug's daddy's (Rev. M. Smith). It was on the east side, off of Alameda Blvd in Los Angeles, CA. Even as a five-year-old child, I can remember loving everything about it.

Seeing my mom and aunts singing in the choir, hearing Rev. Smith pray, preach, and seeing him baptize people was the highlight of my week. Even after all the traumas in my life, I still wanted to be baptized because I desired the

God that I saw my mom praise and desperately wanted that same freedom I witnessed in her. However, my mom, full of wisdom and the fear of the *LORD*, said, "I want you to understand what it is all about before you are baptized. I do not want you baptized because everybody else is doing it. I want you to know why, first."

Consequently, at that time, I was not baptized. Nevertheless, my mom kept me close because she was the parent assigned to nurture me spiritually. My dad had not yet given his life to the *LORD*. His presence as a husband, dad, provider, protector, and disciplinarian played its part in the guidance and upbringing in our home.

As time progressed, I found myself doing well academically. I also ran track and was a captain on the drill team squad that one of my aunts oversaw. I won gold and silver medals for track and field, received academic achievement awards, and had *become* a *Young Black Scholar* by the time I was in the seventh grade of middle school. By the grace of God, I was able to maintain the title *of a Young Black Scholar* until my sophomore year at Crenshaw High School.

Life was good, so I thought. *Then* one day, I believe in December of 1987, while driving home with my mom, we stopped at a red light, and all of a sudden, my mom broke down crying uncontrollably. This time it was just my mom and me in the car. With tears in my eyes, I watched my mom, who was considered the pillar of the family's strength and wisdom, cry all the way home. Because I had never seen my mom cry, I was scared and worried about why she was weeping without reservation. So, with all of the sensitivity and tenderness I had as a teenager, I asked, "Momma, what's wrong?"

A short time later, I was devastated to find out the unexpected news that my mom was given a date and only had a few months to live. Even so, she never missed a beat at home or attending church. She kept taking me with her to church. We would go to different churches periodically to hear various gospel quartette singing groups when they came to town. kept pouring into me and showing me through her example of how to live by faith. *Finally,* on Mother's Day in 1988, I was water baptized. Thank God she was able to witness it.

Unfortunately, on July 30, 1988, a little over two months after the doctors predicted, the summer of my first year of high school, the time when a young lady needs her mom the most, my mom transitioned as a *good soldier*. She was my backbone, my protector, my friend, role model, intercessor, nurturer, the perfect example of a wife, and mother to all seven of her children.

The trauma of losing my mom was painful and devastatingly lonely, even in a house of eight. I wish I knew then what I know now. In this life, we will have trouble (John 16:33). I also wish I knew the scriptures of comfort and relief that I know now. I believe the Word of God could have helped me process my emotions and better prioritize my decisions at that time.

Scriptures like,

> *"Casting all your care on Him; for He careth for you" (*1 Peter 5:7).
>
> *"Blessed are they that mourn: for they shall be comforted" (Matthew 5:4).*
>
> *"Come unto Me, all ye that labour and are heavy laden, and I will give you rest. Take My yoke upon you, and learn of Me;* ***;*** *for I am meek and lowly in heart: and ye shall find rest unto your souls. For My yoke is easy, and My burden is light" (Matthew 11:28-30).*

My humanity said, "It would have saved me the heartaches and heartbreaks of several things if I had known the Word of God better." The divinity *within me* now realizes that,

> *"All things work together for good to them that love God, to them who are called according to His purpose" (Romans 8:28).*

The heartaches and difficulties in life are all a part of *the process of becoming*.

On August 5, 1988, we said our goodbyes to our *beloved* mommy, wife, sister, aunt, friend, and philanthropist. Although it was a somber occasion, it warmed and amazed our hearts to see the crowd of people who came to pay their respects and give honor to my mom. It was extraordinary for me to know that other people could see what we always knew about my mommy.

She was a stay-at-home wife and mother of seven: one boy (the oldest) and six girls. As a stay-at-home mom, you would think we would only have the support of family members, our close neighbors, her siblings, church family, and a few friends. However, this Jewel's life and walk with Christ shined so brightly that it was evident by the standing room only homegoing celebration held at Apostolic Faith Home Assembly, a reasonably large church building. People to whom my mom fed, clothed, housed, and showed kindness were all present at the service. It spoke volumes to me even as a teenager of who she was, not just to her family and friends but also to perfect strangers.

That day, I remember my dad's best friend saying, with his loud voice, "If Rose didn't make it to heaven, ain't nobody going!" Those words still stick with me to this day, over 30 years later. I am sure it was because he, too, recognized that the Christ in my mom did not allow the ups and downs of life to stop her from living life and fulfilling her purpose, and neither should you.

> *"For I am persuaded, that neither death, nor life, nor angels, nor principalities, nor powers, nor things present, nor things to come, Nor height, nor depth, nor any other creature, shall be able to separate us from the love of God, which is in Christ Jesus our LORD" (Romans 8:38-39)*
>
> *"Brethren, I count not myself to have apprehended: but this one thing I do,*

forgetting those things which are behind, and reaching forth unto those things which are before, I press toward the mark of the high calling of God in Christ Jesus." (Philippians 3:13-14)

Stage 1 - When you struggle early on in life, you go through what I like to call the *Eating Stage*. The eating stage begins when life begins to make subtle deposits that serve as life lessons down the line. This stage is a time of growth and mental development when you are drinking the Word's milk, as trusting infants, before eating the strong meat of the Word as mature adults with the capacity to eat the meat and throw away the bones.

BREAKTHROUGH SESSION

The Cocoon Stage - Please take this time to think back in your mind so you can move forward in life by uncovering the deposits made in your life that can serve as beneficial life lessons for you *n*ow. Then, take a notebook or journal and write down ways to implement the lessons for your personal growth and development.

"And we know that all things work together for good to them that love God, to them who are called according to His purpose" (Romans 8:28).

CHAPTER 2

TRANSITION STAGE

After experiencing trauma after trauma, some of us can either get stuck in those moments or drown out those moments by doing things to compensate for the voids left behind by the awful experiences. While others cautiously and with proper guidance, learn to seek a wise counselor or allow God to send wise counselors, all the while trusting God to heal them from the inside out as they go.

My way of dealing with trauma was to look for *love* in all the wrong places. I was so empty that I forgot my role and identity. I was always told how pretty I was as a little girl, so I made myself available for capture to be made to feel pretty. Because I believed what one of my dads' cousins told me at an early age, "You can win over anybody of the male persuasion with those eyes." So, I used what I had—the curves and big brown eyes. Eventually, I became somewhat promiscuous to fill the void of the absence of my mother. If you were my boyfriend, you had just about all of me. The emptiness of living without my mom was so deep that I started *becoming* prey for whatever I thought my man wanted, to get him to "love" me and fill the emptiness I was experiencing. I found out the hard way that once they got what they wanted, I was history. At that time, I didn't know that holding out was best.

My thing or weakness was a deep desire to have a male "love" me. So what thing(s) do you use to fill the void or empty places in your heart? Is it women, men, alcohol, drugs, success, attention-seeking, partying, material things, or name brands? The truth is, only God can honestly fill those empty places and spaces.

I was 16 years old when my mom passed. We never had the opportunity to talk about the *birds and the bees*, and my daddy definitely would not be the one to teach me. Growing up, if my dress was too tight, I had to take it off. I even remember arching my eyebrows at one point without my dad's permission. I had to stay in the house until they grew back. At that moment, I knew Mr. Fleming was not the one to teach me the things that mommy would have taught me to prepare me.

Mister, who I affectionately, respectfully, and jokingly call my daddy, seemed like he would whoop me for anything he thought I was doing wrong. Of course, I appreciate every last one of them now. However, then, I did not understand, and I thought he hated me—another seed of rejection.

> *"Withhold not correction from the child: For if thou beatest him with the rod, he shall not* die" *(Proverbs 23:13).*

My dad apologizes until this day when we reminisce and laugh about the good old days, then he *often* says, "But look how you turned out."

But, despite the fear I had of my dad and his whooping's, from the 11th grade to the 12th grade, both of my older sisters and I heard was, "If you get pregnant, you gotta get out of here! I done raised *all* my kids." So, by the 12th grade, I had two big black garbage bags packed by my room door for two months. Because by that time, I received the news that I was pregnant.

About a year prior, my brother married. Now, he and his wife had their own apartment. So, I had my test results mailed to their address. I thought to myself, "He would never tell daddy I was pregnant." Boy, was I *wrong.*

One day a few of us girls were at home watching T.V., laughing, and waiting for everybody else to come home from school and work. Then, unexpectedly, my dad comes home early from work. He pops in and immediately turns off the T.V. Looking directly at me, he asks, "Do you have anything to tell me?"

"Nope." At the time, I did not because I was

planning to leave *when* he told me. After all, he had drilled it in us his "If…then" statement. In my 18-year-old head, I had it all figured out; my child's grandmother said we could come live with them.

A few days later, my dad comes home again and turns the T.V. off. This time he asked a different question. This time he was straight to the point, "Are you pregnant?" I had to tell him the truth and thank God he did not make me leave. After our short conversation, I quickly unpacked those trash bags, put everything back in my drawers, and was able to take a deep breath—what a relief.

Even though I was five months pregnant when he confronted me, it did not stop me from finishing High School, nor did it stop me from walking across the stage in my cap and gown to receive my diploma while being seven months pregnant. Then, two months later, out comes the most adorably handsome, hazel-eyed, curly-haired baby boy that I have ever laid my eyes on, my *only child, my son!*

Being a single mother and raising my son was one of the most challenging yet rewarding things I have ever had to do in my life. Having to raise an African American son in South Los Angeles was no small task. Mothers can only do so much when it comes to raising boys to *become* men. However, I gave it my *best,* and I encourage all single mothers or dads to do the same. All things are possible with the help of God the Father. There are big brother/sister programs for your sons/daughters *that are* licensed *and* live-scanned. *There are also* qualified ministers within the community of your local churches and community leaders who are willing, able, and certified to help you and give you wise counsel to help you *redirect* your children's steps. Please do not allow yourselves to *become* overwhelmed. Help is available. I know more about the available resources now than I did while raising my son. So, I freely give all that I have learned to you.

Being raised in a single-parent home caused my son to experience his own voids. He wanted to connect and engage, but it was often challenged, which caused him to experience constant feelings of rejection. He was bullied by kids in the neighborhood, at school, and sadly even children within the church. The continuous bullying ultimately provoked him to anger and caused him to learn how to protect and defend himself. He was confronted almost daily and had to fight and stand up for himself. He would always win, but he got *tired* of fighting. Those in the neighborhood just would not stop until he became allies with them.

I would pray and pray and pray and cry out to God for my son daily. Then, one day before leaving 5:00 A.M. morning prayer, I was prompted to put blessed oil on a handful of napkins and ride up and down the streets in the neighborhood, pleading the blood of Jesus and dropping the napkins out of the window as I went. As I prayed, I believed God would steer my son in another direction if he stepped foot on any of those streets. God answered my prayers.

At some point, my son came to himself and realized that his lifestyle was not the life he wanted to live, so he put himself through school and became a truck driver to begin distancing himself from his old lifestyle to create a better future for himself. He traveled out of state days at a time, from one week to the next, making sure he could refocus and prepare for what was on the way. He was about to *become* a daddy.

On August 5, precisely 27 years after the trauma of burying my mom, I became a glam-ma (a young grandmother), and my son had his *pride and joy*—his twin. When his son was born, he said excitedly, "I did not know I could love like this." He loved well. However, due to uncontrollable circumstances, he became both mom and dad. To watch him day and night *transform* right in front of my eyes, loving on and caring for his son, was indeed a blessing for me to watch.

After some time, I heard God say with urgency, "spend time with your son." So, I did. We started hanging out more, going out to eat for lunch, and just taking time to talk! He would talk while I listened. Then, I would speak. He would listen, and we *loved it.* I even moved from my temporary housing to help out and watch my grandson when my son traveled. He did well. Those were proud moments for me to see him grow into fatherhood and be responsible.

Unfortunately, he was estranged from his dad for several years because he was furious about many unanswered questions. Eventually, the unanswered questions drove them apart. Nevertheless, again, out of the blue, my baby wanted to talk to his dad. They squashed their differences, and not long after, he and the baby went to hang out with him for about a month or so. I could see the little boy in my 25-year-old son, who always longed for a relationship with his dad.

Sadly, not long after they returned home,

gun violence took my son, my baby—Champ's dad. Someone took my only child away from us when Champ was only eight months old. What pain! Even amid the pain and agony of having to begin to live a "*new normal*"—without my baby, I learned the necessity of remaining in a place where I can hear from God amid the hurt, the wounds, and vulnerability. In crises, many voices will begin to speak. I had to choose almost moment by moment which voice to follow. I had to learn how to remain in the presence of God, and at that point, it was by-any-means-necessary to keep working towards getting God's *original* outcome for my life in peace.

Even in grieving, some stages lead to healing. First, I had to get past the anger stage and all of the other emotions that came with my loss. Then, I had to learn how to prioritize my feelings because they would begin working like quicksand against me to overtake me and try to pull me down to the point of fatal suffocation.

Thoughts of suicide continuously invaded my mind. Nevertheless, God was my refuge and deliverer.

In your difficult seasons, I encourage you to confront every emotion as they come. Learn to face your feelings immediately so that they will not antagonize you later on in life. Repressed emotions will try to suffocate you by taking your breath, drive, and passion for life away so that you are stuck and lack the desire to *become*. In addition, suppressed emotions cause you to focus more on your pain and not on your process, distracting you from discovering the goldmine inside of you.

In learning to deal with my stifled emotions, I had to cry when I felt like it, talk it out when I needed to, journal, and write it out when I was critical and skeptical of feedback. Words on paper do not talk back. Your loss could be the death of a loved one, a divorce, a job, a house, or a friendship. Whatever you have experienced, unpack your emotions as they come by releasing them all to God first in prayer and then by sharing your feelings with proven and trusted people who can give you wise counsel. When you are vulnerable, you must be extra careful not to give over classified information or receive trash that derails your purpose.

Even though I knew God was my solution, my source for healing, there was a time when I even became angry with God. One day, I heard in my spirit as clear as day, "I am the same yesterday, today, and forever." Then it hit me; God does not change. He is still good and still God. I owe Him despite the struggles I have had. People would say to me just how *strong* I was. The only thing I could tell them was, "Trust me; it is only God. I am not leaning, trusting, or depending on my strength; I have to rely on God." I had to learn how to make God feel comfortable and make Him feel welcomed and wanted in me and my environment. I had to learn how to create an atmosphere for Him because I wanted and needed Him to help me and bring me through every step of that season and every season of my life. In His presence is fullness of joy (Psalms 16:11). I needed it. He is the difference-maker, and He had already proven Himself to me in many ways, so I knew to trust Him to see me through it all, though it was not easy.

My siblings, nieces, nephews, family members, and close friends would all come over, cry, worry about me daily, and wonder how I was making it because of our loss. Even to them, my answer was and is today, "Only God." I am so grateful and appreciative for all of them for caring about us, checking on us, and making sure that we had everything we needed during that horrific time. God bless you.

We have our days and moments, just like anyone else who has faced hard times and losses, but even with those times and in those moments, I have learned that if God is not present with us, we are ships without sails, squirrels without nuts, and books without pages. So, we keep life pushing.

With everything that surrounded me during that time of my life, I realized that I could not afford to forfeit what I had with God based on how I felt at the time. Feelings change. I did not want to risk what I have in Him, based on my feelings or my flesh, by choosing to walk away from what I had known to be in Him—peace, wise counsel, understanding, comfort, and the joy that the world could not give or take away. I had to grow in everything that I was facing to learn that God's presence is heaven to me, that I am safe and secure in Him. I was like a seed in the ground, buried and fertilized to produce much fruit.

In that season of my life, a time of brokenness and vulnerability, I had to learn, have, and depend on the presence of God. *I was becoming* acquainted with God as my Father. I had to learn to let him love me, hold me, teach me, correct me, and tell me that things would get better. I had to trust Him through the process.

The more I would cry out to God in prayer and gravitate towards Him, the more our encounters became about what Abba wanted to reveal to me about me. During this time, he began to show me areas in my life He wanted access to because I needed transformation. He wanted me free to function appropriately in His original intent for my life.

Like Adam and Eve, being in God's presence reveals your true self as undone and total wrecks, with having feelings of unworthiness to even to be called or allowed into His presence. Called to come up higher or to be allowed in His presence—His secret place, a repentant heart that agrees with the will of God is required before deeper access is granted. So, you must know that there is a purpose for being invited into the presence of God. In His presence, God gives assignments, and responsibilities are distributed.

In Isaiah 6:7, a seraph put live coal from the altar, the place of sacrifice, on Isaiah's lips. Why? Because his heart, intentions, and motives were not pure. Accordingly, to activate and make alive that which was in him from the beginning, purification was necessary.

"Then the LORD put out His hand, and touched my mouth. And the LORD said to me, Behold, I have put My words in your mouth*"(Jeremiah 1:9).*

"A good man out of the good treasure of his heart bringeth forth that which is good; and an evil man out of the evil treasure of his heart bringeth forth that which is evil: for of the abundance of the heart his mouth speaketh" (Luke 6:45).

When the seraphim touched Isaiah's lips with the live coal, he was then permitted to speak on behalf of God because his heart was now aligned with God's heart.

When your heart aligns with God's heart,

posture yourself in prayer, position yourself to hear God's instruction, and you meet the *fullness of time,* you will begin to want to say like Moses, "If Your *presence* is not with me, I will not go." Because, in all of your doing, your heart wants to please God.

Moses left the example of the *necessity* of having God's presence and doing things His way. When you understand His teachings, you want to be pleasing in His sight instead of failing Him. When you remain in His presence, you can surrender to His will and produce beautiful results.

Through every difficulty, I have learned that I need the presence and glory of God in my life. I discovered that you get it by submitting to Him, inquiring of Him, listening for His voice in prayer, and realizing that prayer is not a monologue—a one-way conversation; Prayer is a dialogue—a two-way conversation. I speak. He listens. He speaks. I hear and obey His instructions. Speaking and refusing to allow the Father the opportunity to talk back is venting. Prayer is obeying what He entrusts to us. He said that He reveals His secrets to His friends, those who fear and reverence Him, and His to servants, the prophets. God desires a relationship with His friends. "*Oh, what a friend we have in Jesus*."

Furthermore, what a responsibility it is to be considered a friend of God. We cannot take it lightly or wear the responsibilities loosely. "To whom much is given, much is required." So, as we pray and God reveals in prayer and entrusts us with His secrets, we must be willing to obey to get His expected outcome.

> *"For I know the thoughts that I think toward you, saith the LORD, thoughts of peace, and not of evil, to give you an expected end" (Jeremiah 29:11).*

One requirement for Moses was to come out from among them, from among his norm, and from those he was comfortable being around. He did not mind being challenged or stretched to do better and *become* a better leader. Once you accept the calling on your life and begin walking in its fullness for that season, at some point, who knows what will be required of you to gain more in-depth knowledge and revelation of God for the *next* stage.

Some requirements could be that you have to remain single for a while. I have had to stay single for years, and it had *become* like a mockery to me. For years, sermons sounded like they were talking directly to me, "What's wrong with you? It is all your fault! You are too old! Blah, blah, blah." I felt like Hannah being antagonized, provoked, and agitated by Peninnah (1 Samuel chapter 1). I have endured a few snobbish, haughty stares. I have been ridiculed, tolerated, and the topic of catty conversations while trying to cope with my own awareness of being single.

At first, learning genuinely to rejoice when others were rejoicing about getting married, celebrating anniversaries, and going on trips and cruises was hard. Nevertheless, I did it because I learned the importance of planting seeds that would produce a positive harvest for me in the fullness of time. In the beginning, I was in *my feelings*. Listening to the ridicule provoked even more negative thinking, which produced negative seeds, which became harmful fruit. It was unfortunate that my desire to get *married,* not *become* a wife first, was more prevalent and in the forefront of my mind than *becoming* the person necessary to help sustain a marriage!

So, I began embracing my season. I began to seize every moment of my singleness by going to the movies, breakfast, lunch, and dinner by myself. This season helped me to fall back in love with myself. I had to pray *much* to find out my likes and dislikes. I had to figure out what I could and could not stand about myself and what I needed to change. I could not expect anyone else to love what I did not even like about myself.

Even after leading a group that caters to the relationships, I still needed transformation. First, we would meet up together at the beach, coordinated in our well-known "white tops, and jean bottoms" with food, fun, plenty of laughs, and conversations from A-Z. Then, as the sunset, we would gather around the bonfire and talk about things within the group's self-explained title, *Waiting, Dating, and Marriage*. The time of sharing and gleaning was beautiful. Couples, over the years, have given several testimonies of getting married as a result of the group. All glory to God. Still, I was silently frustrated due to my unfulfilled desire to marry. Like so many leaders, I was leading while bleeding.

There were times in ministry where I could be amongst a full congregation and still feel as though I was alone. Yes, some of it was me and my stinking thinking due to the negative seeds planted and immaturely nurtured. These negative seeds bred a mental war within my mind regarding what was versus the promise. This mental warfare is what I call the

Contradiction Factor. However, some of it was God's hand, protecting me from making decisions that would lead to rejection.

I was skeptical of just about anybody who wanted to befriend or get close to me because of my stinking thinking. My first thoughts were, "Who are you? What do you want with or from me? Who sent you?" So, I had often repelled possible destiny helpers, friendships, and opportunities. I avoided them because of the things I had experienced and heard. The hurts, traumas, betrayals, and disappointments caused me to vacillate back and forth, saying, "Do I trust them, or do I continue to hold them at bay?" In the avoidance, I did not take advantage of the seasons to take notes of what I needed to learn and deal with to uproot the negatives and plant the positives for proper growth and development. Instead, I allowed what I wanted to overpower me and lull me to sleep.

"While men slept, his enemy came and sowed tares among the wheat and went

his way" (Matthew 13:25).

You cannot afford to allow what you go through to be so overpowering that it knocks you out and puts you to sleep. So instead, stay woke and fight off the thief of your promise, purpose, and destiny.

I am learning more and more that God wants you and me to be awake and sober so that we are not tricked, distracted, or deceived by the enemy of our souls and get talked out of our birthrights. From day one, the enemy has asked the question, "Did He say?" The enemy of our souls loves to use demonic, subtle suggestions to plant seeds of doubt in our minds to try and make us question the One who knows the way we should take. He is the One who made us. He knows everything there is to know. He is the Counselor whom we can learn to trust. He desires us to take delight in Him while waiting on the manifestations of His promises for us.

God wants us to be the type of fruit that is

palatable, edible, and nourishing for others because anything done in bitterness taints whatever we do. I have personally learned that bitter fruit, for most, is discarded. Not everybody can handle you in the bitter stage, and it is okay. However, God knows what He is doing. Therefore, he always sends expert strategists at the appointed time. He will send those who know how to cultivate, those who are skilled and trained to understand the when and how to handle those in critical stages of bitterness.

Consequently, I had to be alone for a while to see myself, be willing to deal with myself, and welcome the strategists assigned to my life and personal guarded space. I realized then that I needed those living the life, not those who only knew the black ink on the white pages. I needed real help. Head knowledge means absolutely nothing if it is not driven by experience and love, which gives a greater sense of compassion and intensity for the survival and greater good of the person in need.

Being delivered from stinking thinking reinforced my ability to discern. At this point, I believed I could catch my breath, thinking things would get better from here since my discernment had improved. Sadly, there were still layers of healing that I needed from being rejected. In my interactions with people, I would take things personally. I started thinking, "What is wrong with me?" Maybe there is something wrong with me." At that time, I did not realize the spiritual battle that was raging. Subsequently, I began questioning almost everything I did until I heard the Spirit of God say in my spirit, "Do everything you do as unto the *LORD*!" From there, I knew this was the beginning of real healing for mc.

When dealing with the spirit of rejection, it produces various types of *fruit* such as: comparing yourself with others, the inability to believe God, doubt, being *needy*, being a man-pleaser, *becoming* offended easily, *becoming* embarrassed too quickly, feeling alone in a crowd of people, having a superior or snobbish attitude, refusing to admit wrong, and having feelings of hopelessness.

I had *become* so bombarded with wanting to be *accepted and loved* that I started dancing to the beat of others' drums. I could not realize that a rhythm had begun beating inside of me that could only be heard by me first for me to begin to flow in the heartbeat and rhythm of God. I had to let go of being a man-pleaser to fine-tune my hearing. Suddenly, I began to realize something that my mom always told us as we were growing up, "Only what you do for Christ will last."

So, in my *process*, I had to be delivered from the strivings of men (Psalms 18:43) and accept the fact that nobody's perfect, not even me. I realized that we are all works in progress, under construction, and that my job as a piece of God's puzzle in life is to make sure that I do my part so that we all fit to *become* His beautiful vision manifested in the earth.

We fit individually first by being observant

and aware of our weight and shape. Then, with patience, we look at the other pieces of the puzzle's weight and shape. Finally, after thorough observation, we take what we have learned to God in prayer, see what He says about it, and approach the other puzzle pieces with the instructions gained by listening in prayer. Then, we can wisely and lovingly move in the timing of God to begin to see the big picture.

In other words, I had to take myself out of the picture (my feelings, emotions, my flesh), pray, and intercede. Then, I entered the darkroom to view the negatives accurately to come out with a clearer perspective. I needed to see how God sees things; after all, He created me. He knows just how each part is supposed to operate.

In *the process of becoming* God's original intent for your life, there will be a series of dates and events that either has happened, is happening, will happen, or that will need revisiting to gain the knowledge, wisdom, and skill intended for you to learn to succeed during the transitional times of your life. You may have missed it in times past, but I pray now that you have gained some helpful insights and strategies so that when the fullness of time comes for you to *become*, the wisdom, love, and presence of God will lead you to victory. In my darkest hour, each word God gave me served as a stone to step out on as I walked, trusting Him by faith.

God is amazing. Even in our processing seasons, he will ensure that we *become* so that we are sustained and equipped to enjoy His purposed life for us freely.

Stage 2 - The time when it seems like all hell is breaking loose. This stage is the phase when it looks like nothing you do seems to work. During this period, you do not know whether to stay or walk away. Why? Because it is in these times, we are building the spiritual muscles necessary to break through your cocoon.

The Transition Stage - Think about and write down some of the most challenging times that you have experienced, along with things you discovered about yourself and where you found strength during your process. Then, praise God and pat yourself on the back for enduring the process.

> *"And not only so, but we glory in tribulations also: knowing that tribulation worketh patience; And patience, experience; and experience, hope: And hope maketh not ashamed; because the love of God is shed abroad in our hearts by the Holy Ghost which is given unto us." (Romans 5:3-5).*

CHAPTER 3

THE PRODUCTION STAGE

"And as He prayed, the fashion of his countenance was altered, and his raiment was white and glistering" (Luke 9:29.)

"He answered and said, Lo, I see four men loose, walking in the midst of the fire, and they have no hurt; and the form of the fourth is like the Son of God. Then Nebuchadnezzar came near to the mouth of the burning fiery furnace, and spake, and said, Shadrach, Meshach, and Abed–nego, ye servants of the most high God, come forth, and come hither. Then Shadrach, Meshach, and Abed–nego,

came forth of the midst of the fire" (Daniel 3:25-26).

So, Shadrach, Meshach, and Abednego came out of the fire, and the people crowded around them. They saw that the fire had not harmed their bodies, nor was a hair on their heads singed; their robes were not scorched, and there was no smell of smoke on them.

After years of serving in the ministry of prayer and intercession, standing between the problem and solution, doing all I could to *become*, and attempting to stay clean in God's sight in order to qualify to come boldly before Him in prayer on behalf of others, I fought many battles. I have come through countless fires to learn to endure as a good soldier because I desired to be found faithful.

There are times when you can be so focused on your assignments that you miss the friendly fires of those *working* alongside you. Some individuals God intentionally blocks. Then, there are other battles that you will have to face, confront, and fight. However, if there is no battle, there will be no spoils. It is in those times that you need to be aware of your surroundings, keep your eyes and ears open to the heartbeat and mouth of God, discern well, learn what spirit is in operation, put your weapons (the Word, prayer, worship, and faith) in one hand, and keep serving and doing what you are called to do in the other hand like in Nehemiah 4:17,

> *"They which builded on the wall, and they that bare burdens, with those that laded, every one with one of his hands wrought in work, and with the other hand held a weapon."*

The work you are doing is too important. To *become*, you must have a nevertheless inside of you!

> *"Saying, Father, if thou be willing, remove this cup from Me: nevertheless, not my will, but thine, be done" (Luke*

22:42)

In the *process of becoming*, there will be obstacles that will come your way to try to block you from seeing what is written concerning you or oppositions sent to try to intimidate you into backing down from your God-ordained assignment so that *another spirit* contrary to the will of God can take over. So, be wise as a serpent and harmless as a dove to preserve what is at stake—the will of God. That takes courage and boldness. In my family, I am, what they call in my family, a bit *height-challenged*, so I do not back down easily. Thank God for holy boldness. As it is in the natural realm, so it is in the spiritual realm. So, I stood tall in standing to maintain my assignment.

During a particular time in this process, there were moments when I prematurely wanted things that interfered with my ability to hear and see God. So, my ability to choose accurately and wisely was almost impossible. I have always been so hard on myself until I found out that even Jesus struggled within Himself when He said, *"If it be possible, let this cup pass from me" (Matthew 26:39).* So, I pressed.

It is human nature to want to dodge pain and suffering. However, there are some things that we must face during the process before becoming that will be hard to confront, things that we would rather skip. Nevertheless, like Jesus, we must realize that Father knows best, and all things are working together for our good. It is your responsibility to submit with a nevertheless to learn that every sacrifice required of you to *become* God's original intent for your life. Your life is for you and those who are assigned to you. Remember, there is always a reward and purpose on the other side of your pain and obedience. You have to learn to trust God with your very life. There will be glory after this.

> *"But, the God of all grace, who hath called us unto his eternal glory by Christ Jesus, after that ye have suffered a*

while, make you perfect, stablish, strengthen, settle you" (1 Peter 5:10).

Remember, after Jesus said, "*Let this cup pass from me*," an angel came and strengthened Him. You must remember that there will be times when the battles are hitting hard and frequent that you want to give up during your process. There will be times when you will want to throw in the towel. I tried throwing in my towel. However, he threw it back at me by reminding me that His strength is made perfect in my weaknesses.

You cannot do His next level in your own strength. You will not win holding on to something God requires you to let go of. Do not *become* like Achan, who took the accursed thing (Joshua 7:1). Whatever God wants from you, surrender it to him, so you can crossover into what God has for you. The next level requires purity, holiness, righteousness, freedom, and liberty because this is the level you will have to forgive and deliver your enemies, even when it hurts.

A former bishop of mine once said during one of his sermons that certain things are attached to a rocket when it launches to help the rocket take off. However, as it reaches a certain altitude, the same parts needed to launch the rocket must detach and fall off so that the rocket can reach its encoded destination. Although that was many years ago, it was a great illustration and impartation that has helped me through many seasons of my life. So, as God began to mature and elevate me in areas and things began to happen to, and for me, because of God's anointing, people began to fall off, it even became a bit chaotic, but I have learned that God creates order in the midst of chaos. So, the oppositions were necessary for me to gain spiritual muscle and fortitude.

During my *process of becoming*, I could not stop moving forward because God would not let me. Instead, he gave me a desire, a grace, and a willingness to *evolve*. I had to count all as dung to get to know God and what He wanted me to learn of Him during that season of my life. In pursuit of Him and my purpose, my name was changed to Hephzibah, meaning my delight. God took me from being rejected by man to *becoming* His delight. Who would not serve a God like this?

So, in challenging seasons, learn to trust God to make your face as hard as flint, keep your eyes fixed and focused on the prize, and to press into the assignment even more as unto God and not unto man or woman. Now, when you serve, do not allow man's issues to *become* a weight that slows you down or brings your process to a halt.

Joseph had been dumped, left for dead, and then sold into slavery by his brothers. Those he felt closest to betrayed him because they envied him because of the dream he was carrying. After a series of events, he was promoted from the pit to the prison and finally to the palace and given authority. Joseph is a great example to follow. He never stopped being who he was or doing what God called him to do. He was faithful, even in the midst of being confined and limited. As Christians, you will have to have it in your heart to say, "Father forgive them for they know not what they do." Had Christ chosen to give up the ghost with unforgiveness or hatred in His heart towards His haters, His sacrifice would not have been acceptable, and the outcome would not have been to the saving of souls. His nevertheless was needed for our salvation, so your "nevertheless" will also save lives.

So, even though at this level, things are difficult, there is purpose in your pain. It may be painful, but it is needed because the fullness of time requires you to push. Your push will birth you into the glory intended for your life.

Suppose you purposely choose not to stay focused on your assignment but the daggers or those throwing them. This shift in concentration could not only abort and forfeit the best of who you are to *become*, but you could also cause a generation of people to abort, relinquish, or delay b*ecoming* their best as well. So, pray, and resist the spirit of fear (false evidence appearing real), and begin to renounce and denounce selfishness, anger, bitterness, unforgiveness, the spirit of rejection, and anything else that could be festering within your hearts that could cause you to fall short of the glory of God. Continue to feed your spirit man with the Word of God and be transformed in your mind. Your ability to overcome will help free you to *become*.

Often, God uses challenging situations to develop character and then requires a withdrawal from what He has deposited on the inside of you. He uses specifically skilled workers to help assist in the provocation and activation of the person you already are in the spirit to help you face the more sensitive and difficult places. Sometimes it will come by way of specific instructions that you must be willing to follow to *become* and fulfill your calling as he did with Abraham in Genesis 12:1,

> *"Now the LORD had said unto Abram, Get thee out of thy country, and from thy kindred, and from thy father's house, unto a land that I will shew thee."*

There were no specific instructions. Just go.

> *"Take now thy son, thine only son Isaac, whom thou lovest, and get thee into the land of Moriah; and offer him there for a burnt offering upon one of the mountains which I will tell thee of" (Genesis 22:2).*

Then there are times when God will give specific. Just obey, no questions asked. Only trust him. The time came for me to do just that after serving in a ministry, Vision Int'l Ministries, for over 13-years, under the leadership of two influential people, who helped me unlearn some things so that I could relearn the true principles of the Word. After being in church for many years, they retaught me principles found in the

Word and principles about prayer. Bishop William P. Morgan and Dr. Sarah Morgan, whom I honor and value today for pouring into me the Word of God, from a place of passion, wisdom, knowledge, love, revelation, and compassion until I owned it. Up until that point, I had never experienced such a powerful way of teaching.

Although I was learning and maturing in the things of God, in obedience, my pursuit began. First, I went to several churches looking and listening for the voice assigned to me for my next season. Then, I heard the voice and the sound in Apostle Veronica C. Moore in a place that I was familiar with—the place of prayer, which is the place of power. After that, I experienced powerful encounters every week at the Altar of Prayer.

Sadly, because there is a tendency to compare apples and oranges when we are moved from one place to another, I fell into that trap. Unconsciously, I began to compare, and I was blocking my opportunity for a fresh outpouring. There is one body but many members. Each part doing its part must be honored, valued, and respected for the body to function properly and reproduce after its own kind. I learned from my mistake. So, when God leads you to a new place, please go with an open mind. Test every spirit to see if they are of God and move accordingly. Have a teachable spirit so that those God has sent to help you can fulfill their assignment. When God leads you to a militaristic Apostle/Prophet and Pastor as your leaders, that is when you know that it is time for you to have your boots on the ground in a new capacity.

Transformation, metamorphosis is never easy; it requires work. It would be best if you kept at the forefront of your mind that it is always necessary to do the work. It is just like someone who has enlisted in the army. You enlist, go through Bootcamp, and start from scratch; as a private (E-1) entry-level. During Bootcamp, you learn the ropes. As you are doing your time, you are being tested and observed. Eventually, your captain promotes you to a higher rank if your skills are impeccable or outstanding in His eyes (Captain of Heavens' Army). You will continue to move up in rank as long as you stay enlisted, and this is what I believe happened for me when God said to go. He took me from one level of service to another because He knew that there were areas in my life that had developed and other areas that needed to be developed for me to function in my calling correctly.

God's leading indicates what He is trying to activate in you and where you are being deployed for active duty. Here is where intense warfare begins. Why? Because in this stage, everything about you must change. There must be a complete metamorphosis. In this place, God is commanding the Egyptian mindset and mentality (the negative attitudes that developed throughout the years of testing, trials, disappointments, silent frustrations, unresolved issues) to dissipate. Victory in this area will help you not take it with you into God's next for your life and keep you from walking in the flesh. When there is a real transformation, you can be of help and not to the detriment of others or yourselves. In the place of elevation, you must travel lightly to get the job done effectively.

Leaders know the time of your affirmation and when to release you for active duty. Even when you think you know better, you do not. Humble yourself and sit until you know you are ready and your leaders affirm the calling. Do not get mad. If you do, take it to God in prayer. Remember, it is your character that He wants to develop.

I have faced many different challenging situations in my lifetime: accidents, being held at gunpoint, chased by a loose bull in my childhood neighborhood, being mishandled, openly shamed by those in leadership positions because of assumptions, lied on, and even jailed for three or four days.

Sadly, I was truly innocent. I was not even home when whatever happened, happened. Even so, the police took my sister and me to the police station in separate cars. They handcuffed me and put me in the back of the car while my dad and son looked on from the house. Before pulling off, I heard my son say, "My mom is gonna pray her way out of there!"

I spoke in tongues from the time I sat in that cramp-legged backseat, all the way there. It seemed as if the ride was far, but it was only a few blocks away. Then, finally, the female cop asked, "Are you okay? Are you on any meds/drugs?" I can laugh about it now, but then it was no joke. Little did she know, I was sending an *S.O.S. to* my heavenly Father to go before us to make every crooked path straight, every rough place smooth, level every mountain, and fill every valley. The prayers were to ensure that we were going to be okay when we got there.

While entering the jail station, the other detainees began asking, "Why are you here?" I said sharply, "nothing!" After all, the movies tell us that if we go soft, we will get bullied. So, I had to act a bit tough to back them up.

Their response was, "Yeah, that's what we all say!"

My little sister had gotten sick shortly after they booked us and put us in that small cold cell together. *Won't He do it?* After a while, they came to take her to the "big house" in downtown Los Angeles, where they have a medical facility, but I prayed! When I finally looked back up, she was being brought back to the cell. Before it was all over, they had called most of the women out to form a line to get bused to court while my little sister and I, along with one or two others, were left sitting and waiting. Before the officers called out other names, a young lady who had heard me praying several times throughout this ordeal approached me. She asked, "Are you the one that be in there praying?"

"Yes," I answered.

She said, "Well if there is a God, He's one

mean &#%!@?!" It sparked a conversation. I gave her a Bible and a verse and told her to try Him one more time. She did; she took it and then began to express her fear of going back to court and possibly being sentenced this time. She also started to try and teach us the "ropes" of the system in return. She said, "If they call your name, you are going to court. If they do not call your name, your case is going to be a *DA reject*, and you will go home." Others were listening. One had murdered her friend due to drug use. Another one was detoxing from meth, and others were there for credit card fraud. There were people from all walks of life there. As they called names, our names were not mentioned, neither was the name of the one who had questioned me earlier, "If there is a God..." God answered more than one of my prayers. That day I prayed with her, and she became a believer. By the grace of God, we never went to court, the police dropped the charges, and we went home.

With all of that, I have had people turn others against me. I lost my *only* child and became homeless. God told me, then, that I was on display. I heard in my spirit, "How you go through will determine how long you go through."

Stage 3 - In stage three, trust the *LORD* with all your heart and lean not to your understanding to birth true humility. Here is when everything is in disarray, and nothing seems to make any sense. Stage three is the time of maturation. Here is when we gain spiritual muscles and the ability and confidence needed to fly and reproduce.

BREAKTHROUGH SESSION

The Reproductive Stage - Write down experiences that have humbled you. What was your frame of mind at the time? How has your thinking changed? Write down areas in your mindset that still need processing and make the adjustments.

"For whosoever exalteth himself shall

be abased; and he that humbleth himself shall be exalted" (Luke 14:11).

CHAPTER 4

PROCREATION TIME

In life, you never know who is watching, listening, taking notes, or secretly admiring you from afar. It is best to do the best you can to sanctify yourselves so that those who are watching, listening, taking notes, and secretly admiring you will get *100%* on their tests. Leading by example teaches them to learn from your failures and successes, so keep in mind that transparency in this stage is essential.

Being wise and transparent is noteworthy. You must discern well and know who genuinely needs the help versus those who want *the personal informatio*n that could be used against you later on. Discern well.

When you are an open book while doing what you are called to do, it exposes others' intentions. When it does, remain silent. Say absolutely nothing to the other people involved. Instead, take everything to God in prayer to keep a *pure* heart and clean hands. Be advised in prayer and by the Word of God. Then, wait patiently and prayerfully on God's timing to speak regarding what He reveals and move accordingly. Be obedient from the time He reveals a matter to you until He tells you to release what He has shown you. Also, try to remember that He is preparing their hearts to receive the correction, the rebuke, or your exit. Either way, do it all from a place of love allowing nothing to weigh you down. You have a destiny, and you need to be free enough to flow, fly, and sow seed whenever and wherever you are required to plant to reproduce.

In the previous chapter, I mentioned how a rocket needed certain things to help it get off the ground. However, once it reaches a certain altitude, certain parts are no longer required and discarded so that the rocket can reach its destiny. The same is true for you. The pruning seasons are designed to cause you to produce. Remember, your fruit, what you have to offer, must be palatable and edible for others to consume.

At times, you may look at the losses as a bad thing. However, sometimes your losses are for your good. As a servant of the *LORD*, it is also for the good of those to whom you are assigned. It is crazy how what took us fifteen years to get out of; God will use our experiences and wisdom gained from it to get a perfect stranger out of their situation in fifteen minutes. Would you say it was all worth it to see their relief and release? For some, if not all, I know it will take time to say yes without hesitation because of the fear of reopening old wounds, but as God continues to give opportunity after opportunity to help others, it *becomes* a relief and a release for us as well. Each option, your yes, no, or maybe all, stretches your faith, even when you do not fully understand so that you will become.

As I stretched my faith and went when I heard in my spirit to do so, God confirmed his Word. I continued to sit in the audience until I was identified, called forward, anointed and affirmed the leader and prophet God told me I was many years ago. I am finally free enough to be able to say and accept it now. I used to run from my calling. However, God reminded me of the generations waiting for my voice and His words. The weight of my responsibility increased, and so did the calls, text messages, and in-boxes from people who began to place a demand on what God deposited inside of me. The fullness of time had come.

The enemy of your soul will always try to make you abort your *becoming* so that you never *become*. The enemy will use your history of weaknesses, failures, and shortcomings to make you feel like you are not qualified to be used by God. In contrast, the trials authenticate the call and assignments.

"But I have prayed for thee, that thy faith

fail not: and when you have converted, strengthen your brethren" (Luke 22:32).

Anything inside of you that is lying dormant and not yet submitted to God, the enemy will use against you as you progress and approach your moment of *becoming*. When whatever has been lying dormant awakens, it returns with great vengeance to try and make you abort and forfeit your destiny. More resistance is needed here. The enemy does not want you to *become*. He knows that the butterfly season is where you will get more done and do more damage to the kingdom of darkness than you could stuck and bound in your cocoon.

When you are in the process of *becoming*, the enemy will dangle your desires before you like a carrot to try to force you to give up your birthright and abort your destiny. We must deal with those desires before they deal with us. In James 4:7 it says,

"Submit yourselves therefore to God. Resist the devil, and he will flee from

you."

Jesus was taken to a high mountain, and there was asked in Matthew 4:6-7,

> *"And saith unto Him, If thou be the Son of God, cast thyself down: for it is written, He shall give His angels charge concerning thee: and in their hands, they shall bear thee up, lest at any time thou dash thy foot against a stone. Jesus answered him, It is written again, Thou shalt not tempt the LORD thy God."*

The Word of God is a weapon against the enemy, and you must learn how to use it properly—rightly dividing the Word so that you may *become* polished arrows in the hand of God. Then, you can walk in liberty and victory. As we submit to God, He gives us the strength to deal with ourselves first, and then with everything and everyone else, so that the enemy will flee from us.

You have to intentionally decide within to

obey God in everything you say and do. If you disobey Him once you know what to do and say, you cause others to miss out on what you are designed to impart into them, and you miss out on the blessings that come from your obedience. Having head knowledge will only lead to stagnancy. Allowing God's Word to *become* both spirit and life brings with it the ability, confidence, and power to do what is being asked or commanded of you and gives birth to what has been read in the Word and spoken over you through prophecy. We gain those results and blessings by *receiving* and ingesting the Word of God. We are to consume it and be consumed by it to *become*.

There were several times throughout this process that I thought a particular person, place, or thing was a *God thing* that turned out to be *a my thing*. It was something or someone that I wanted that was not necessarily who or what Abba wanted for me. Thank God for the teachings I had received during my earlier walk with the *LORD* that taught me always to endeavor to make an indelible mark on the lives of anyone I was privileged to come in contact with. It made it much easier to weather the storms of having to let go of my things. Again, I did not always get it right, but I obeyed what I believed was right at the time until God revealed His truth concerning the matter at hand, and a decision had to be made to choose otherwise. Although I felt like a failure because *my* plans did not always work out, the deposits were well worth the lessons that thrust me forward towards God's original intention for my life.

As I mentioned earlier in this chapter, those you are assigned to and those given to you are looking and taking notes on what you say and do. Remember to keep deciding daily to do life and ministry the way God has written for you. Your tribe is waiting for you to *become* God's original intent for you so that their hope and faith will increase, and let them know that if He did it for you, He can and will do it for them.

My *becoming* has not been smooth sailing, but how else do we get oil out of olives without the crushing and the pressing? It is painful yet necessary. How else do we get a skilled worker without the worker humbling himself to be taught to apply the teachings effectively? How else does a wounded woman *become* a lady and then a wife without going through relationally, correcting a wrong self-image, learning from bad choices, and choosing to remain vulnerable even after being hurt over and over again? It is all necessary for the process of *becoming*. The process equips us so that we are sustained and useful in that ordained place to get optimal results for ourselves and those we are called to serve. Service, not being served, is the highest seat in the kingdom. To lead well, you must first serve well. *"The greatest among you shall be your servant"* (Matthew 23:11).

During your process, with or without a title, serve. With or without the fame, fortune, accolades, or opinions of men, serve.

Obedience to the voice of God has its mental and emotional pros and cons. You will feel like you are on an emotional rollercoaster because you are not exempt from the mental and emotional battles. However, you have to decide that obedience is better than sacrifice. Take the bitter with the sweet and serve in the capacity you have been processed in to *become*.

> *"But the God of all grace, who hath called us unto his eternal glory by Christ Jesus, after that ye have suffered a while, make you perfect, stablish, strengthen, settle you" (1 Peter 5:10).*

You have been restored, confirmed, strengthened, and established. Now fly.

Stage 4 - In *stage* four of *becoming,* you do what you were called and created to do without past limitations or restrictions. Phase four is when you press in unselfishly by identifying yourself with your I AM statement. I AM declarations allow you to speak over yourself and rehearse what has been prophesied over your life. Then, you operate in your I AM statements without apology, in humility, while feeling honored to be called into a place of service to your tribe.

Remember, all things are working together for the good of them that love God, who are the called according to His purpose. So, endure the process and *become* God's original intent. You deserve it, and your tribe is waiting.

Breakthrough Session

The Procreation Stage - Think about the things you have suffered. Then, listen to Holy Spirit for insights regarding what you are called to do and who you are to *become*. Write down everything Holy Spirit reveals to you and find scriptures that will give you an understanding of your purpose. The insights and scripture will *become* your strategy in prayer on your path to destiny.

> *"Moreover it is required in stewards, that a man be found faithful" (1Corinthians 4:2).*

"I press toward the mark for the prize of the high calling of God in Christ Jesus" (Philippians 3:14).

"Be not afraid of their faces: for I am with you with thee to deliver thee, saith the L*ORD" (Jeremiah 1:8*

ADDENDUM

EYE, THE BUTTERFLY

by Clint "Saint Ice" Johnson

I came out of my cocoon too soon.
My wings were not strong enough to carry me.
I don't wanna rock with a bunch of caterpillars,
but I'm not ready to fly.
Oh, I'm just a boy with butterfly wings, dangerous.

I want to fly so bad.
Want to lift off and ascend, not depending upon the
wind and accolades of the voices of the masses,
even the drama masks of the few.

So, I feel quarantined, locked down, plugged into
my source, of course.
I'm experiencing transformation enveloped in my
consecration,
My concentration in my elevation back into my
chrysalis--maturing enduring.

I need my wings to be stable, able to move abundant
weight, mine, and the burden of others, those that I
know love for and care for.

Filtered, sheltered from the sun's rays, tones of shades, more than watercolor, my pallet is cool-idascope, created like no other to fly and float to splash in torrent or ease as the breeze...to breathe,

As a man, the male butterfly, you won't see me cry, never catch me falling,
It's my calling to navigate the thin line between love and hate, so in my cocoon, I wait, waiting for the power of my wings to carry the weight, to escape the caterpillars.

As if atmospheric re-entry into the womb, so I'm back into my cocoon, to fail again?
I cannot afford, again affixed to an umbilical cord, while sharpening my sword.

Now I'm in my cocoon until the day my wings can carry me.
All that I dare to be care to be is dangling in front of me.
No more caterpillars, it's now or never, my blade cuts and severs-

The pains of change uttering, stuttering my spirit shuttering being birthed for better in the protective casing my heartbeat pacing accelerating, racing.
What is this?

No more wishing or pretending wings extending fluttering metamorphosis.
I began to pant nearly rant in the rhythm of a chant
I will; I shall, I will, I shall, As the silky cocoon

unfolds like a birth canal.
I beckon the direction- push into the opening,
I can do it-uh, get through it-uh, life's fluid gushing
all over me.

The old man vanished, for flight I am famished, the
transformation has taken over me bonding,
responding to the cooling calming airstreams.

See my beautiful, powerful wings lifting me beyond
what I used to be embracing my royalty.
I majestically fly, glide in the skies
now I see what I was created to be.

Eye the Butterfly

ABOUT THE AUTHOR

Sylvia R. Fleming, a.k.a Lady Sylvia, is a willing vessel, prophetic intercessor, ordained minister, daughter, granddaughter, grandmother, sister, cousin, niece, a licensed hairstylist—on and off screens and stages. She is the founder of *Waiting, Dating, and Marriage* and a Word of Fire Tabernacle Church member under Pastor Calvin and Apostle Veronica Moore's leadership.

Because of the things she has suffered: kidnapping, the loss of her mother and untimely death of her son, rejection, and homelessness, she has dedicated her time and life to encouraging and providing help, hope, and guidance to those who find themselves in similar situations, with the hope that they too will experience the freedom and liberty to *become.*

CONTACT INFORMATION

Ladysylviathe1@gmail.com

SOCIAL MEDIA

Facebook @TheProcessofBecoming

Instagram @the_processofbecoming

Made in the USA
Coppell, TX
21 November 2021

66172877R00059